THE SC
BOOK O

WEATHER

Dr Anthony Wilson is a writer and teacher who started his career sending weather balloons up into the ozone layer. He went on to be Head of Education at the Science Museum in London, where he set up the popular hands-on gallery *Launch Pad*. He has lived in Tonbridge, Kent, for many years, but wasn't there in July 1868 when Britain's highest-ever temperature, 38.1°C or 100.5°F, was recorded just a few hundred metres from where he now lives. (Unfortunately this record is now regarded as a bit suspect.) His favourite sort of weather is a mild westerly autumn gale.

Many of the amazing facts in this book were inspired by exhibits in the SCIENCE MUSEUM in London. It is home to many of the greatest treasures in the history of science, invention and discovery, and there are also hands-on galleries where you can try things out for yourself. If you live in the North of England visit the Science Museum's outposts, the National Railway Museum in York and the National Museum of Photography, Film & Television in Bradford.

Published by Hodder Children's Books 1999
The right of Anthony Wilson to be identified as the Author and the right of Sean Longcroft to be identified as the Illustrator of the Work has been asserted by them in accordance with the Copyright, Designs and Patents Act 1988

10 9 8 7 6 5 4 3 2 1

A Catalogue record for this book is available from the British Library

ISBN 0 340 73624 0

Designed by Fiona Webb
Cover illustration by Ainslie MacLeod

Hodder Children's Books
A division of Hodder Headline plc
338 Euston Road
London NW1 3BH

Printed and bound in Great Britain by
The Guernsey Press Company Limited,Guernsey,C.I..

THE SCIENCE MUSEUM
BOOK OF AMAZING FACTS

WEATHER

ANTHONY WILSON

ILLUSTRATED BY SEAN LONGCROFT

Hodder Children's Books

a division of Hodder Headline plc

Stormy weather for another three weeks...

Contents

DANGER
RAINWATER

CHAPTER 1

Weather watchers

Weather affects our lives in many ways – where we live, what we wear, when we go on holiday. Perhaps that's one reason we talk about it so much. For some people weather even brings their lives to an end, if they die in a storm or flood, or 'catch their death of cold'.

In the old days weather was even more important, when most people lived in the country and did their work out of doors. They learnt to do their own forecasting, with the aid of rhymes such as 'red sky at night, shepherd's delight'.

Soldiers and sailors have always had to watch the weather, too. Bad weather has often upset their best-laid battle plans, changing the course of history as a result.

It has taken a long time for scientists to learn how to produce better forecasts than ordinary people can. But official forecasts are much better now than they were a few years ago, and are still improving. Modern weather forecasting is a high-tech business, relying on satellites, balloons, high-speed communications and some of the most powerful computers in the world.

WEATHEROLOGY

Planetologists study the planets, futurologists predict the future, and gemologists are experts on gems, but meteorologists don't study meteors. In the old days the word 'meteor' was used to describe anything unusual that came from the sky, including rain, snow and flashes of lightning, as well as the streaks of light that are sometimes called shooting stars. Today we only use the word 'meteor' to describe the high-speed grains of rock that hit the Earth from outer space and produce shooting stars. But just to be confusing we don't give the name 'weatherologist' to the scientists who study rain, snow and everything else to do with the weather. Instead we still call them 'meteorologists'. And what do we call the scientists who really do study meteors? They're just ... astronomers!

FIRST FORECASTER

The first official weather forecaster in Britain, Robert Fitzroy, killed himself after *The Times* newspaper stopped printing his forecasts because they were inaccurate. Fitzroy was an admiral in the Navy, who had earlier been

Uh-oh...
wrong
again!

captain of the ship in which the famous naturalist Charles Darwin sailed around the world. He made his forecasts using weather reports from observers around the country. These reports were sent to him on the newfangled electric telegraph – the first-ever device to send messages instantly from one place to another. But at that time no one understood the way weather systems work, so Fitzroy's forecasts weren't very good. This disappointment, together with other problems, led to his tragic suicide in 1865.

SAINT ALEX

When Alexander Buchan's weather predictions turned out correct, a newspaper suggested he should be made into St Alexander, the patron saint of weather. Buchan was a Scottish schoolmaster who in 1867 pointed out that in Edinburgh certain dates during the year tend to be warmer than usual, and others tend to be colder. At first he had a run of successes, but then his luck turned and it became clear that his predictions were no better than anyone else's. Even so, Buchan did much useful work as a meteorologist, including helping to start a weather station on the top of the mountain

Ben Nevis. But the honour of being patron saint of weather belongs to several other people.

WATCH THE BIRDIE

Some people predict the weather by watching birds and animals. For example they say that if a robin sings in the low branches of a tree, then rain is on the way. But if it sings high up in the tree the outlook is for fine weather. A bird called the Storm Petrel even got its name because it's thought to be a good weather-forecaster. It normally flies far out to sea, but when a storm is near it will come in closer to the shore. But don't rely on cows for your forecast. Apparently the old idea that they lie down when it's going to rain just isn't true. If cows lie down it means they've finished eating grass and need to spend some time digesting it.

WARNED BY WORMS ...

A 'Tempest Predictor' worked by worms was put on show in London in 1851. The miniature forecasters inside this gadget were actually leeches, which are fat worms that look like slugs and have the nasty habit of sucking blood out of whatever they attach themselves to – including humans. Apparently leeches keep still in fine weather, but get much more active when a storm is coming, and have been used a lot in China for forecasting rain. The 'Tempest Predictor' was invented by the well-named Mr Merryweather and consisted of twelve glass jars, each with a leech inside. When bad weather was near, the leeches were supposed to climb to the top of their jars. This made a little bell ring, to warn the owner to take his umbrella when he went out. Mr Merryweather tried to persuade the government to set up a chain of 'leech-warning stations' around the country, but with no success.

... AND OTHER CREEPY-CRAWLIES

If you don't have any leeches handy, you can try using other creepy-crawlies as your personal forecasters. Here are a few old rhymes that tell you what to look for: 'When black snails on the road you see, then on the morrow rain will be', 'When the glow-worm lights her lamp, the air is always damp', and 'If spiders their cobwebs forsake, the weather for certain will break'. And if you can't find any snails, glow-worms or spiders, try counting woodlice; another old tale warns that if you see a lot of woodlice running about, it will soon be raining. There's often a grain of truth in these old sayings – people in the old days lived much closer to nature than we do, and were better at noticing small signs that warn of changing weather.

INSECT THERMOMETER

When you want to know the temperature, ask a cricket! Crickets are insects similar to grasshoppers, often found in warm places. They make a regular chirping noise, and the hotter it is, the faster they chirp. One type, the snowy tree cricket, is so reliable it's sometimes called a 'thermometer cricket'. To find the temperature (in °C), just count how many times one of these crickets chirps in 25 seconds, add on 13, and divide the result by 3. The reason it works is that crickets, like all insects, are cold-blooded – so their body temperature is the same as the temperature around them. On cold days all their body processes run slowly, including chirping, but as the temperature rises, everything speeds up. One expert claims you can also find the temperature by measuring how fast ants walk.

THE ONION TEST

To find which months will be wet in the year ahead, why not try the Onion Test, used in France in days gone by? All you have to do is put twelve onions in a row, to represent the months from January to December. On Christmas Day put a pinch of salt on top of each onion. Then leave them alone for twelve days. On 6 January look for onions where the salt is still dry; these tell you which will be the dry months in the coming year. But beware of onions where the salt has 'melted' – according to the old story, these will be the rainy months. Don't use this method if you're choosing when to take your summer holiday; it's one of many old beliefs that don't have a grain of truth in them.

IN THE DOLDRUMS

When someone looks miserable we sometimes say they are 'in the doldrums'. The phrase used to apply to sailing ships in a region near the Equator where very little wind blows. It was called the 'doldrums', and sailors dreaded going there, because there was so little wind their ships got stuck there. So the ships, and the sailors, were said to be 'in the doldrums'.

We use a few other everyday words and phrases that originally come from talking about the weather, such as 'He got a frosty reception', 'I was thunderstruck', 'She has a sunny nature'. You may be able to think of some more, particularly if your brain works at 'lightning speed'.

SUNNY BIRTHDAYS

If your birthday is in the summer you're likely to get better presents than if it's in the middle of winter. This very unfair arrangement is caused by sunshine.

Researchers have discovered that when the sky's blue and the sun is shining people feel more cheerful (as if we didn't know that already). People also give bigger tips in restaurants and buy better presents for their friends. They are more friendly and less likely to complain when things go wrong. They even buy more cars and houses in sunny weather. Perhaps this also means that people in Britain give smaller Christmas presents than people in Australia. In Britain, Christmas is often cold and dull. But in Australia 25 December is in the middle of summer.

SAD WINTERS

Some people are made seriously ill by the gloomy weather we get in winter. The illness is called SAD ('seasonal affective disorder'), and may affect about one person in twenty, making them feel sluggish and depressed. No one is sure why people get this illness, but one theory is that when there's a shortage of sunshine a gland in their bodies produces too much of a special substance that lowers their mood. The problem is often worse for people who live in northern parts of Europe where the winter days are short and the nights long. People who suffer from SAD often feel better if they spend half an hour a day sitting under a bright lamp that imitates sunlight.

POISONOUS WEATHER

First your fingers and toes feel icy cold and then they feel burning hot. Then they shrivel and drop off. That was one effect of a horrific disease that affected thousands of people in cold damp weather hundreds of years ago. At that time people usually made bread from rye, instead of the wheat that we normally use today. If the weather was cool and damp when the rye was harvested, a deadly fungus called 'ergot' would get into the rye and make the bread poisonous. The ergot poison was similar to the modern illegal drug LSD, so that as well as affecting their fingers and toes, eating poisoned rye bread gave people hallucinations – they thought they could see strange and amazing things that weren't really there. Many people died from the terrible effects of eating poisoned rye bread. Luckily bread made from wheat doesn't have the same problem.

NAPOLEON MEETS HIS WATERLOO

The result of one of the most famous battles in history was decided by the weather. On the morning of 18 June 1815, the French general, Napoleon Bonaparte, was ready to attack the massed armies of Britain and other countries, under the Duke of Wellington, at the small Belgian town of Waterloo. But Napoleon made a fatal mistake. Instead of starting the battle straight away, he waited until noon. This allowed time for another fighting force, of Prussians, to arrive and join the battle on the British side. Many historians think that the

Prussians tipped the scale in Britain's favour. Without them, Napoleon might not have lost the Battle of Waterloo. Why did he make the fatal mistake? Because it rained so much the night before, so Napoleon allowed time for the ground to dry out before starting the battle. Defeat at Waterloo brought Napoleon's career to an end.

'GENERAL WINTER'

Waterloo wasn't the first time Napoleon was defeated by bad weather. Two years earlier he led an army of 600,000 men into Russia to attack Moscow. But as winter approached many of the French soldiers died from cold and lack of food. The rest had to trudge back to France through the depths of the bitter Russian winter. With no other food available, they even had to cut pieces off their horses to eat – but the horses didn't notice because they were numb with cold. From the whole of the army, only 20,000 men survived. Napoleon wasn't too bothered that he had been defeated by 'General Winter'. 'A man like me is not much concerned over the lives of a million men,' he said.

WAR WEATHER

One of the greatest battles of the twentieth century was launched by weather-forecasters. They didn't actually start the battle themselves, of course, but the general in command waited for a good forecast before sending his troops into action. It happened in 1944, near the end of the Second World War, when German troops were still in control of France. A huge armada, with more than 2000 ships and 150,000 soldiers, was waiting in England to cross the Channel to France to drive the Germans out. At first bad weather held up the invasion, but on 5 June forecasters predicted that the following day would be calmer. Relying on their prediction, General Eisenhower, supreme commander of the invasion force, gave the go-ahead. Happily the forecast proved correct, and the invasion, codenamed 'Operation Overlord', got off to a successful start.

POTATOES AND THE PRESIDENT

If it hadn't rained so much in Ireland in 1845, Bill Clinton might never have become President of the United States. At that time most people in Ireland relied on potatoes as their main source of food. Disaster struck in 1845 when the summer was so cool and wet that a disease spread through the potato crop and made all the potatoes rot in the ground. About a million people died in the famine that followed. In the following years millions more left Ireland for good, and started new lives in the United States. Among them were some people called Cassidy, and President Clinton is one of their descendants. It all goes to show how much the weather can affect the course of history.

GREEN FLASH

You've heard of a 'blue Moon', but what about a 'green Sun'? It does happen, but very rarely. Just occasionally, when the Sun is rising in the morning, the first glimpse you get of it may be a green flash that lasts a second or two, before the main part of the Sun comes into view. And when the Sun sets at night you might see the green flash again, just as the last bit of the Sun disappears over the horizon.

These green flashes are caused by the way the Sun's light is bent by the air (in the same way that a glass lens can bend light). The light is split into rainbow colours, and the green part may be the first to appear at sunrise, or the last to disappear at sunset. But very few people have ever seen the green flash, because it only happens 'once in a blue Moon' – and requires very clear, still air.

ALL IN THE MIND?

Ships mysteriously floating in the sky, and camels upside down in the desert. Do people really see these things, or are they just visions that come to people when they're dying of thirst in the desert? The answer is that these sights, called 'mirages', do really happen. Sometimes the Sun heats up the surface of a desert so much that the layer of air next to the surface begins to behave like a mirror. Then you may see things near the horizon, such as distant camels, reflected in this mirror. Light rays also get bent when they pass over cold sea water, so that ships that are really over the horizon look as though they are lifted up into the sky. You can sometimes see a mirage much nearer home: when you're driving on a motorway on a hot day and the road surface ahead begins to look shimmery and like a pool of water.

FORECASTING BY NUMBERS

Before computers were invented, it would have needed 64,000 people, all working flat out with mechanical calculating machines, to predict the next day's weather. In 1922 a British meteorologist, Lewis Richardson, showed how a scientific formula could be used to calculate how today's weather would turn into tomorrow's weather. But when he tried it out, he found it took him six months to do all the maths needed to predict the weather just six hours ahead – and even then his forecast wasn't very accurate! So he realised he would need an army of assistants to keep up with the real weather. By the time Richardson died, in 1950, electronic computers were coming along that could do the job fast enough to be useful. But even today some of the world's most powerful super-computers have to be pressed into service to predict the weather before it actually happens (*see* **Teraflop**).

TERAFLOP

It sounds like a prehistoric animal, but a 'teraflop' is actually a way to measure the power of a super-computer. 'Tera' means 'million million' and a 'flop' is a calculation, so a 'teraflop' computer is one that can complete a million million separate calculations every second. Weather forecasters in Britain's Met Office expect to be using their first teraflop computer by the year 2002. Back in 1998 they still had to make do with a computer that could only manage 400 thousand million calculations a second. Instead of having just one 'processor' in it, like an ordinary home computer, this machine had more than 600 processors all

working away at the same time. The teraflop computer will be the most powerful number-cruncher of all time – and quite a change from 50 years earlier, when the Met Office got its first electric calculator, capable of just one calculation a second.

WEATHER FROM ORBIT

In 1957, one artificial satellite orbited the Earth. Today there are more than 2000 of them. Some of the largest and most important are the weather satellites, which save money and lives by helping forecasters predict hurricanes and other weather hazards well in advance.

Weather satellites do much more than just send back pictures of clouds. They can measure the temperature down below, during the night as well as in daylight, using detectors that pick up infra-red rays. They can also 'see' the difference between damp air and dry air. Often the images from satellites are given false colours by computer, which picks out the details and makes them look more dramatic on the TV weather forecast.

SEEING THE WIND

The latest weather satellites can reduce seasickness by 'seeing' how hard the wind is blowing near the Earth's surface, even though they are looking down from a height of 800 kilometres. They do this over large areas of the oceans where there is no other way of measuring the wind. The cunning gadget that achieves this is called a 'scatterometer'. It sends radio waves down to the sea's surface and measures how they are scattered back up again. From this it can work out how rough the ocean surface is, and that depends on how hard the wind is blowing – more wind means rougher sea. Wind measurements from the scatterometer can be used to warn ships to keep away from stormy regions, which is why the new satellite is particularly popular with people who get seasick when their ship gets into rough water.

RUNAWAY BALLOON

In 1998 Canadian scientists had to call in the Air Force to shoot down one of their own weather balloons. The balloon was as tall as a 25-storey skyscraper – much larger than the hundreds of normal weather balloons that meteorologists send up every day. It had been sent into the upper atmosphere to make measurements in the ozone layer (*see* **Safety shield**, *page 42*), but the automatic system to bring it back to Earth didn't work. Big balloons don't go pop like little ones, and 2000 shots from fighter planes had little effect on it. After drifting thousands of kilometres across the Atlantic Ocean, the runaway giant finally came to Earth in Finland.

WRISTWATCH FORECAST

By 2010, you'll find out whether you need an umbrella by looking at your watch. By then computers might be wristwatch-sized. So you'll be able to get weather-radar pictures for your local area from the Internet and display them on your watch-screen. Weather radar picks up rain, snow and hail. By making several pictures into a movie you can see how fast the weather is moving and work out when it will reach you. By 2020 computers will probably be so clever that you'll just say to your wrist-watch 'I'm going out for half an hour' and it will reply 'Take your umbrella' or 'No need for umbrella' as the case may be.

HOLIDAY WEATHER?

It may never be possible to make detailed weather forecasts more than two weeks ahead – even with an ultra-powerful computer. The problem is that to predict the weather far ahead we need to know every small detail of the weather today – the position of every cloud in the sky, the strength of every gust of wind, and so on. It'll never be possible to measure all these things very precisely, so forecasts far ahead won't come out right in every detail. Meteorologists say this is because the weather is a 'chaotic system'. But reliable *general* forecasts may be possible one day, such as 'next August will be hotter than usual', or 'April next year will be very wet'. These will come in handy when you're booking your holidays. (*For the forecast for thousands of years ahead, look at* **Chilly Outlook?**, *on page 121.*)

Quiz

1 Meteorologists are scientists who
a) Watch for meteors
b) Forecast the weather
c) Do taste-tests on hamburgers

2 Which of these did Robert Fitzroy *not* do?
a) Try to forecast the weather
b) Make a round-the-world voyage
c) Invent the electric telegraph

3 Leeches are slimy creatures which
a) Suck blood
b) Drop dead when it's going to rain
c) Paint their toenails

4 A cricket is an insect that chirps faster when
a) It snows
b) England win a Test Match
c) The weather warms up

5 What are The Doldrums?
a) A place where it never rains
b) A place where there isn't much wind
c) An Indie band from Hartlepool

6 Napoleon delayed starting the Battle of Waterloo because
a) The wind blew him off his horse
b) The ground was too wet
c) It was too foggy to see the enemy

7 The illness SAD is caused by
a) Going out when it's full moon
b) Not seeing enough daylight
c) Watching too many forecasts on TV

8 What is a teraflop?
a) A dead tortoise
b) A comfy chair
c) A lot of sums

9 Weather satellites are launched into space to
a) Beam back weather images
b) Broadcast disaster movies
c) Block out the sunlight

10 Long-term forecasts may never be accurate because
a) Computers break down too often
b) The weather is too chaotic
c) Forecasters aren't paid enough

CHAPTER 2

Thin Air

We often forget we all live at the bottom of an ocean of air – the Earth's atmosphere – which presses down on us in the same way that water presses down on deep-sea divers. Scientists began to understand about air pressure more than three centuries ago. Later they worked out that normal air is a mixture of gases.

Air always contains much the same amount of some gases, such as oxygen and nitrogen, but the amount of some other gases varies. On warm damp days there's quite a lot of the invisible gas called water vapour, but much less when it's cold and dry. When the water vapour turns back into liquid water we see it as clouds. Two other gases, carbon dioxide and ozone, play an important part in the way the atmosphere works, but the amount of both of these has been changed by human pollution.

The atmosphere is a skin of gas all round the Earth, just a few hundred kilometres thick. It's thin but vitally important. You can think of it as a sort of theatre-stage, where all the drama of the weather is played out.

HEAVY AS AIR

The total weight of air pressing down on your head and shoulders at this moment is about one tonne – the same weight as an average-sized car. It just goes to show that air's not as light as many people think. In fact normal atmospheric pressure produces a weight of about one kilogram pressing down on every square centimetre. Air pressure squeezes us on all sides, not just from above, but we don't get squashed by it because our bodies are pressurised inside. If air pressure changes slightly we may notice the difference because our ears 'pop' or begin to hurt. A big change in air pressure can cause major problems, as three Russian astronauts discovered when their space capsule sprang a leak and lost pressure in 1971. All three were dead by the time the capsule landed back on Earth.

MOUNTAIN-TOP SCIENCE

A famous French scientist got his brother to carry a barometer to the top of one of the highest mountains in Central France. The experiment was thought up by Blaise Pascal in 1648 and its aim was to show that air has weight. A barometer measures the weight of air above us. Down at ground level there's a lot of air on top of us, so the air pressure is high. At the top of a mountain there's less air up above, so the air pressure gets less – like when a deep-sea diver comes up nearer the surface. Pascal got his brother (who lived near the mountain) to take readings of the barometer at the bottom and at various stages up to the top. The result was exactly as predicted and helped to convince people that we really do live at the bottom of an 'ocean' of air.

TUG OF WAR

In 1654 the mayor of a small German town harnessed the power of sixteen horses to show how strong atmospheric pressure is.

The mayor, Otto von Guericke, used a hollow metal ball, just 50 centimetres across, which was cut in half to make two hemispheres. He put these hemispheres face-to-face and used a pump to take out the air from inside. He found that the hemispheres were then squeezed together so tightly by the pressure of the atmosphere on the outside of them that a tug-of-war between two teams of eight horses failed to pull them apart. The German Emperor came to watch this demonstration of air pressure and was amazed by what he saw.

TONGUE-TWISTER

One of the gases in the atmosphere was given the name 'dephlogisticated air' when it was first identified in the 1770s. Luckily this tongue-twisting name was soon changed to a simpler one, oxygen. One of the discoverers of oxygen was an English clergyman, Joseph Priestley. As well as being a scientist, he had advanced ideas about freedom and religion which so upset local people that they completely smashed his house and lab in Birmingham. Oxygen makes up about one-fifth of the air we breathe. The rest is largely another gas which was originally known as 'azote' but is now called 'nitrogen'.

KRYPTON FACTOR

'Krypton' isn't only a word in the title of a TV show, or even the name of the planet where Superman was born. It's also the name of a gas that we breathe all the time. In an average roomful of normal air, there's enough krypton gas to fill a matchbox, but it's invisible and has no smell, so it's very hard to tell it's there. Breathing it doesn't do us any harm – or any good. Krypton gas is used inside some fluorescent lamp tubes, and in some photographers' flash guns. Several other harmless gases are mixed in with normal air. One of them, xenon, is a hundred times rarer than krypton.

MICKEY MOUSE GAS

One of the gases in the atmosphere makes your voice sound like Mickey Mouse. It's called 'helium' and makes up just one part in 200,000 of normal air. If you separate out the helium from the rest of the air, and take a deep breath of it, your voice comes out very squeaky even when you try to speak normally. This is because sound waves travel much faster in helium than in normal air. But it's dangerous to breathe pure helium for more than a second or two because it cuts off your body's oxygen supply. Helium gas is important for weather-forecasters because they use it to fill the balloons that carry their measuring instruments into the upper atmosphere.

INVISIBLE DRINK

On a hot and humid day in summer there could be enough invisible water in your living room to fill three normal-sized drinks cans. The invisible water is called water vapour, and it's mixed with the air that fills the room. You can't see the vapour but you can tell it's there by putting something cold in the room, such as a glass of cold drink. Cool air can't hold as much water vapour as warm air, so when warm air touches the cold glass some of its vapour turns back to liquid water on the outside of the glass. Have you ever noticed the same thing happening when you open the door of your freezer on a sticky summer's day? This time the vapour turns back into tiny drops of water which form a small cloud of mist.

SALTY TALES

There's some truth in the old joke that forecasters rely on a piece of seaweed to help them predict the weather. Some seaweed contains a chemical that takes in water from damp air. If you hang up a piece of the seaweed it will feel dry in fine weather. But when the air is damp the surface of the seaweed will begin to feel sticky. So seaweed tells you when the air has more water vapour in it, which means clouds and mist could form, and rain may not be far away. In the old days, ordinary salt had a similar property. In damp air it went sticky and wouldn't pour out of the salt-cellar properly. But today the salt has chemicals called 'anti-caking agents' in it to stop this happening.

METEOROLOGISTS PREFER BLONDES

Did you know that your hair is longer on a damp day than on a dry one? On damp days hair takes in water from the air and expands. On dry days it loses water and goes back to its original length. This has been used to make instruments, called hygrometers, which measure how humid the air is. A length of human hair inside the instrument is wrapped round a small wheel. On damp days the hair expands and turns the wheel, making a pointer move towards the 'wet' mark on the dial. Apparently blond hair works best, but the natural oils have to be taken out. But if you've got a hygrometer at home it may not have hair inside it; some of them use bits of cow's intestines instead!

SAFETY SHIELD

Dangerous rays from the Sun would harm almost every living thing on Earth, if we weren't protected by a layer of ozone gas no thicker than a biscuit. Ozone is a special form of oxygen which lets through ordinary sunlight but acts as a shield to block out ultraviolet rays which can cause skin cancer and other problems. Without the ozone layer the only really safe place for animals and plants to live would be underground or deep under water, and people would have to put on sunblock cream whenever they went out in sunlight. (Actually the ozone gas isn't in one thin layer, but is mixed in with the ordinary air of the upper atmosphere, about 25 kilometres above our heads. But if we could collect all the ozone together it would make a layer about 3 millimetres thick.)

HOLE IN THE SKY

When British scientists discovered the famous 'ozone hole' in 1982, they could hardly believe it themselves. So they waited two years before going public with their results. By then they were sure that the 'hole' was real. What they discovered wasn't really a hole at all, but a patch of sky near the south pole – about the size of North America – where the ozone layer gets much thinner than usual at certain times of year. Scientists think the hole is caused by pollution from gases called CFCs, once used in refrigerators and spray cans, which escape into the atmosphere and eat away at the ozone gas. To stop the hole spreading, different gases are now used in refrigerators and spray cans, but it could be at least a hundred years before the ozone layer fully recovers.

BLANKET OF GAS

If all the carbon dioxide gas in the atmosphere was collected into a single layer, that layer would now be almost 3 metres thick. A hundred years ago it was a lot thinner, but it's now growing thicker by about an extra 5 millimetres a year, mainly because of all the extra carbon dioxide people make by burning oil, gas, petrol, wood and other fuels. In fact every time you switch on a light or go out in a car you add a little bit of extra carbon dioxide. Actually the carbon dioxide is mixed in with the other gases in the air, but you can think of it as forming a blanket round the Earth. This helps to trap the Sun's heat, and is the reason everyone is so worried about the 'Greenhouse Effect'. Experts aren't sure just what effect the thickening blanket will have, but it could change the Earth's climate in disastrous ways (*see* **Global chilling**, *page 122*).

DEADLY FOG

In 1952, 12,000 people were killed in London by fog. In those days many homes were heated by coal fires which gave off a lot of smoke. In

December 1952, the weather was unusually calm, so the smoke built up instead of blowing away, forming a smog (combination of smoke and fog) that lasted for several days. The smog was so thick you couldn't see more than ten metres in any direction. Breathing the evil-smelling smog was difficult, and many people with heart and lung problems died. Soon afterwards, new laws were passed to stop people burning smoky coal in London and other cities, so deadly smogs like the 1952 one don't happen any more.

BREATHING DUST

In a busy city, you could breathe in a hundred million specks of dust with every breath you take. Out in the country the number is lower – only five million dust grains in every breath of fresh air on average. Most of the dust grains are too small to see, and cause little trouble because you simply breathe them out again. Larger ones can get stuck in your lungs and cause problems such as hay fever, asthma, and other serious diseases. The grains come from smoke, traffic fumes, factory machines, pollen from plants and even from distant forest fires and volcano eruptions. Household items like cushions and blankets also give out a lot of dust; you can sometimes see it dancing around in a beam of sunlight.

BREATHING ATOMS

There are ten thousand million million million atoms in every lungful of air you breathe – or 10,000,000,000,000,000,000,000 if you prefer it written in numbers. If you tried to count them all, starting now and counting at the rate of one every second, it would take thousands of billions of years – which is much longer than the age of the universe. But if everyone on Earth helped you with the counting you could get the job done in only 50,000 years. Of course scientists don't really have to count atoms one at a time to find out how many we suck in with every breath. They can calculate the answer using ideas worked out by a German chemist called Joseph Loschmidt in 1865.

CAESAR'S LAST BREATH

On 15 March of the year 44 BC, the famous Roman emperor Julius Caesar was murdered. Where are all the atoms today that were in Caesar's last breath, just before he died?

Amazingly, thousands of them are in the same room as you at this moment. After Caesar died it took a few years for the wind to spread all those billions of his last-breath atoms around the world and mix them in with the rest of the atmosphere. Because most of the air is nitrogen gas, and nitrogen only gets used up very slowly, most of Caesar's last-breath atoms are still around today. In fact, there's probably an atom from Caesar's last breath in every breath you ever take.

BREATH OF FRESH AIR?

It isn't just an atom from Caesar's *last* breath that's in every breath you take. There's probably one from his next-to-last breath too, and every other breath he ever took. In fact in the same room as you at this moment there could be atoms from every breath ever taken by everyone who ever lived on Earth – apart from a few recent breaths that haven't had time to get mixed in yet. This is almost impossible to believe, but you'll have to try very hard, because the calculation has been done many times, and the answer always comes out the same. Sadly, all nitrogen atoms look exactly the same, so even if you had a super-microscope there's absolutely no way you could tell which atoms are the ones that were once breathed by Julius Caesar, or Joan of Arc, or Adolf Hitler, or Marilyn Monroe, or your own great-grandmother, or anyone else.

LIQUID AIR

If the Earth was as cold as the planet Neptune, the atmosphere would turn to liquid. Instead of the atmosphere being a layer of gas more than 100 kilometres thick, the frozen Earth would be covered by a layer of liquid air just 10 metres deep – enough to submerge an average two-storey house. But don't worry; for the atmosphere to turn to liquid the Earth would have to cool to about - 200 °C, and the sun's heat will stop that happening for at least the next five billion years.

Quiz

1 We don't get crushed by the pressure of the air because
a) Air pressure is extremely weak
b) The air doesn't press on living things
c) We're pressurised inside as well

2 In the famous experiment in 1654, what tried to pull apart two hemispheres?
a) 16 horses
b) 8 elephants
c) 2 steam locomotives

3 Oxygen was once known as
a) Discombobulated gas
b) Dephlogisticated air
c) Unadulterated bilge

4 Which of these can helium *not* be used for?
a) Filling weather balloons
b) Making fizzy drinks
c) Imitating Mickey Mouse

5 People use a piece of seaweed to forecast the weather because
a) It starts to smell when the air pressure falls
b) It blows away when it's windy
c) It feels sticky when wet weather is approaching

6 Which of these might you *not* find inside a hygrometer?
a) A length of hair
b) A bit of cat's whisker
c) A bit of cow's gut

7 The Ozone Hole is
a) A famous night-club in Berlin
b) An expensive brand of perfume
c) Something in the sky over Antarctica

8 The 'Greenhouse Effect' means the Earth may get warmer because
a) So many people now have central heating
b) So many people now have greenhouses
c) Extra carbon dioxide gas acts like a blanket to trap heat

9 The dreadful London smog in 1952 was mainly caused by
a) Too many coal fires
b) Too many people smoking
c) Too many bonfires

10 Atoms from Caesar's last breath are now in the same room as you because
a) There were billions of them and they've got mixed in
b) Caesar took enormous breaths
c) Caesar died near where you live

CHAPTER 3

Going to Extremes

Weather enthusiasts love to say things like 'Yesterday was the third hottest Thursday in September since 1887'. They know it's true because thousands of weather stations around the world make regular measurements every day, and all these measurements are stored on computers. We even have measurements from times before proper meteorology got going, because people sometimes kept diaries in which they noted down the weather.

Keeping detailed weather records helps meteorologists make better forecasts. It also lets them pin-point the real record-breakers – times and places where the weather goes to world-beating extremes.

Some of the most amazing weather freaks, like giant hailstones or record snowfalls, are not recorded by weather experts at all – just by ordinary people who happen to be in the right place at the right time.

Now that spacecraft visit other parts of the solar system, scientists have discovered other worlds – planets and satellites – that break the weather-records set on planet Earth.

DEATH BY HAILSTONE

The biggest hailstone ever recorded fell at a place called Coffeyville in Kansas, USA, in 1970. It was a ball of ice 14 centimetres across, which is a little wider than the page you are reading now, and it weighed as much as eight copies of this book. Melted down, the stone produced enough water to fill two normal-sized Coca-Cola cans. Farmers dread the sort of storms that bring hail, because a sudden burst of hail can destroy their crops in just a few seconds. Large hailstones also break windows, dent cars and injure people. In America, hail does a billion dollars-worth of damage every year. And in China in 1986 a single hailstorm killed 100 people, injured 9000 and destroyed 35,000 homes.

DRY TOWN

If you go to the town of Arica, in Northern Chile, don't bother to take an umbrella. Arica is the driest town in the world, with an average of less than one millimetre of rain a year. You would have to live there for a thousand years to collect as much rainwater as an average place in Britain receives in one year. The years 1903 to 1917 were particularly dull ones for the man who checks the rain-gauge every day in Arica, because it never rained at all during that period. Surprisingly, there's no shortage of water in the world's driest town. The trouble is it's all salty – Arica is a seaside resort! Lack of rain does have one advantage though. Northern Chile is a good place to see the stars, and astronomers are building a group of enormous telescopes there.

HOT SPOT

Think of the hottest day you've ever experienced in Britain. Now add another 20 °C on top of that. That's how hot it was in the Libyan desert on 13 September 1922, when the temperature reached a world record of 58.0 °C (136 °F). Humans can survive at such a high temperature, but only if the air is dry – as it always is in a desert. In dry air we can easily lose surplus heat by sweating a lot. The sweat quickly evaporates from our skin, and cools us down in the process. Hot and humid places are much more dangerous. When the air is very moist, sweat stays on your skin and doesn't evaporate. Then there's a much greater risk of your body overheating, leading to possible 'heat-stroke'.

DANGEROUS STROKES

Just four degrees can make the difference between life and death – if it's your body temperature we're talking about. If you're in a hot and humid place, and your body temperature goes up by only 4 or 5 °C from its normal 37 °C, you could be suffering from heat-stroke. If it's not treated quickly, this could lead to brain damage and even death. Signs of heat-stroke are when someone stops sweating properly, looks flushed, their heart beats extra fast, and they get confused or even pass out. Treatment starts by cooling the victim down, using wet blankets and fans. You don't have to go out in the sun to get heat-stroke, but in bright sun there's another danger – sun-stroke. This is another dangerous condition that can develop when your skin is damaged by exposing it to an overdose of the Sun's ultraviolet rays.

WETTEST DAY EVER

Imagine a whole year's supply of rain falling in just 24 hours. That's what happened at a place called Aurère, on the island of Réunion in the Indian Ocean on 15–16 March 1952.

In just 24 hours of continuous downpour a total of 1.58 metres of rain came down, which is more than falls on most places in Britain in a whole year. It was the wettest 24 hours ever recorded anywhere on Earth, with more than a tonne and a half of rainwater landing on every square metre of ground. The cause of the drenching was a tropical cyclone which battered the island that day.

FLOOD DISASTER

Bad weather led to the deaths of almost a million people in China in 1887. The disaster happened when heavy rain made the Huang He River overflow its banks. An area the size of England was flooded. Many people drowned and others died from illnesses caused by the flood or from lack of food because crops were washed away. The Huang He River is nick-named 'China's sorrow' because it causes so many flood disasters. As recently as 1998, 14 million people in China were made homeless by floods. Part of the trouble is that the Chinese have cut down millions of trees. This means heavy rain runs straight into the river instead of soaking into the soil. Also more soil getting washed into the rivers clogs them up.

GET SHOVELLING!

Most people get excited when it starts to snow, but how would you feel if 193 centimetres of snow fell in just one day? That's what happened at a place in Colorado, USA, in April 1921. Imagine digging your way out of your house after that snowfall – into a bank of new snow deep enough to cover the head of an average-height adult. But that's nothing compared to the total snowfall recorded at a Ranger Station in Washington State, USA, in the winter of 1971–72. The total snowfall that winter was 28.5 metres. If none of it melted or evaporated, that would be enough to completely cover a ten-storey building.

BITTEN BY FROST

It was so cold in Moscow in December 1993 that 60 people had to have parts of their body cut off. They were victims of frostbite, which is a dangerous condition that happens when parts of the body, such as fingers, toes, ears or nose, get so cold that they actually freeze. Ice crystals forming inside the body damage the flesh, and unless the frozen part is quickly and carefully thawed out, the damage can be permanent. You can even get frostbite without knowing it, because the affected part goes numb with cold, so you can't feel that it's getting frost-bitten. In the worst cases the damaged part never recovers and has to be amputated (cut off by a surgeon). That's what happened to the unfortunate Russians in 1993. More than 40 other people were even worse off; they died of cold in the same icy spell.

GIANT SNOWFLAKES

Snowflakes as big as saucers fell on a town in Hertfordshire, England, in 1951 – but not many people saw them because it happened at 4.30 in the morning. Giant fluffy snowflakes have been observed in other places too. Scientists think they form when smaller flakes begin to stick together. As soon as one flake gets larger than the others it falls faster, sweeping up more and more flakes and growing larger and larger until it hits the ground. In 1887 a country postman in Montana, USA, saw enormous flakes falling that were 38 centimetres across and 20 centimetres thick. Fields for miles around were covered in white spots as the giant flakes landed.

BEWARE OF THE SNOW-EATER

In parts of Canada the temperature can rise by more than 20 °C in just a few minutes, changing winter to spring in less time than it takes to grill a hamburger. It happens when a warm wind suddenly starts to blow down from the Rocky Mountains. Native Americans call this wind 'chinook', which means 'snow-eater', because it makes the snow disappear so quickly. But the chinook can stop as quickly as it starts, plunging the countryside back into bitter winter weather. A similar warm wind sometimes blows in parts of Europe, where it's called the 'föhn'. It's said that the sudden change in temperature can bring health problems, such as headaches and heart attacks, and sometimes even makes people commit suicide.

WIND OF DEATH

You are 64 per cent more likely to get murdered in Los Angeles when the Santa Ana wind is blowing, than when it isn't. Like the chinook, the wind they call the 'Santa Ana' is a hot dry one that comes down from the mountains, and it makes Los Angeles people bad-tempered and edgy. In the old days when murderers were arrested they sometimes tried to get let off by saying they couldn't help themselves because the Santa Ana was blowing. In cities around the world, the police know that any very hot spell puts up the crime rate.

WET AND DRY

The wettest town in Britain gets four times as much rain as the driest town. Fort William in Scotland is at the foot of Britain's highest mountain, Ben Nevis. When moist air comes in from the west, it has to rise up over the mountains, and this makes it cool down and drop its moisture in the form of heavy rain. So enough water falls on Fort William in an average year to cover the town to a depth of two metres. That's four times more than the year's rainfall at Thurrock in Essex, which is on the dry eastern side of the country. But Fort William does get one advantage from all its rain; it was the first town in Britain to run its street-lights by hydroelectric power – electricity produced when rainwater rushing down a mountainside turns a turbine wheel.

WASHOUT

Six million tonnes of water fell on London in less than three hours one afternoon in August 1975 – enough to provide a year's supply of drinking water for everyone in London. Seventeen centimetres of rain fell in the wettest area that day, so if you'd climbed into an empty bathtub in your garden when the rain began, three hours later you'd have been sitting in enough water to have a reasonably deep (but chilly) bath. Unfortunately downpours like this don't fill the city's reservoirs because most of the water runs off down the drains and into the River Thames. Steady gentle rain is much more useful because it sinks in. Then underground rocks soak up the water like sponges and hold it in reserve for Londoners to use later on.

WARMEST WORLD

Which is the hottest planet in the solar system? Many people say Mercury, because that's the closest planet to the Sun. But they're wrong, because Venus – number two from the Sun – is even hotter. This is because Mercury has no atmosphere, but Venus has a very thick one. It's a hundred times heavier than the Earth's atmosphere, and acts like a blanket to keep the planet warm. You couldn't walk about on Venus because its 470 °C surface is so hot your boots would melt or catch fire. And the weather there is terrible. The Sun never shines because it's cloudy everywhere all the time, and some scientists think it rains a lot there too – except that what falls from the sky on Venus is not nice cool water but boiling hot sulphuric acid.

FROZEN MOON

If you think it's cold at the South Pole on Earth, try going to Triton, one of the moons of Neptune. When the spacecraft Voyager 2 flew past Triton in 1989 it measured the temperature of the moon's surface to be -235 °C – only 38 degrees above the coldest possible temperature. Triton is the coldest place in the solar system, although the distant planet Pluto is probably almost as bad. Triton's atmosphere is very thin, because gases like nitrogen and oxygen freeze solid at such a low temperature. But Triton is not a completely dead world; Voyager discovered strange eruptions happening on its surface.

FLYING BACKWARDS

The wind blows so hard on the planet Neptune that a normal jet plane trying to make headway there would actually move rapidly backwards. Even the supersonic Concorde would seem to be hovering as it battled against the ten-times-hurricane-force winds. (Actually there would be a lot of other problems if you tried to fly a jet plane on Neptune; for example there's no oxygen in Neptune's atmosphere so a jet engine wouldn't work at all.) Neptune's winds blow at speeds up to 2000 kilometres per hour in whirlpools in the planet's atmosphere, making it the windiest place in the solar system. Scientists are not sure what causes these amazing winds.

WIND IN SPACE

Even though there's no air in space, a strong wind blows there. It's called the solar wind and it consists of streams of tiny particles, smaller than atoms, shooting out from the Sun. In the region of space near the Earth the solar wind blows at about 500 kilometres per second, which is ten thousand times faster than the fastest winds on Earth. And just as a normal wind makes the smoke from a chimney blow away in a long stream, so the solar wind blows the gas from a comet out into a long tail that always points away from the Sun. Engineers have even designed special spacecraft with huge sails that could be blown through space by the solar wind.

Quiz

1 The largest hailstone ever recorded was about as big as
a) A small pea
b) A strawberry
c) A large grapefruit

2 Northern Chile is a good place to
a) Sell umbrellas
b) Build telescopes
c) Grow rice

3 In the Libyan desert the temperature has reached
a) 38 °C
b) 48 °C
c) 58 °C

4 In the wettest 24 hours ever recorded, how much rain fell on every square metre?
a) A gallon and a half
b) A tonne and a half
c) We don't know because the rain gauge overflowed

5 In 1993 more than forty people in Moscow were killed by
a) Cold
b) Smog
c) Too much vodka

6 What did a country postman see in Montana, USA in 1887?
a) Giant hailstones
b) Giant snowflakes
c) Giant pandas

7 What is the 'föhn'?
a) A warm wind in parts of Europe
b) A cold wind in the Rocky Mountains
c) Something we answer when it rings

8 Where is the wettest town in Britain?
a) Near a river in Essex
b) In a valley in Wales
c) Near a mountain in Scotland

9 The coldest place in the solar system is
a) On one of Neptune's moons
b) In a crater on the Moon
c) Crewe railway station on New Year's Eve

10 Jet planes would fly backwards on Neptune because
a) The pilot would get space sickness
b) Neptune spins the wrong way
c) It's very windy there

CHAPTER 4

What goes up must come down

The Earth's atmosphere is really a huge machine for transporting water around. It starts with the invisible process called evaporation, when the Sun's heat lifts water up into the atmosphere, mainly from the surface of the oceans.

We can't see the water in the atmosphere until it turns into clouds, which are simply enormous collections of tiny drops of water. By the time clouds form, the water is well on its way to the next stage – falling back to Earth as rain, snow or hail. In the end, much of the water runs back into the sea, ready to start the whole process all over again.

For a long time scientists found it hard to explain just why and when water vapour would turn into clouds. And they've had very little success in their attempts to make clouds form to order, when someone down below wants it to rain, and to stop them forming when rain is not wanted.

WATER, WATER EVERYWHERE

Enough rain falls on the Earth every day to provide 200 cubic metres of clean fresh water for every person on the planet. That's enough to let everyone fill an average bath-tub to the brim several hundred times over every day!

So why is there a 'water crisis' – a desperate shortage of clean water in many countries of the world? One reason is that rainwater is hard to catch; much of it soaks into the ground or runs away, soon becoming polluted and perhaps carrying diseases. Another is that much more rain falls in some regions than others, and people in dry countries can't afford to have water tanked over from countries where there's water to spare. Much of the world's fresh water supply is needed for irrigation (watering crops). So when water is in short supply, people in dry countries don't just go thirsty; they may starve as well.

RAIN COLLECTOR

The first scientist to regularly measure rainfall started in 1677 and didn't miss a day for the next 26 years. He was Richard Towneley who lived in a grand hall in Lancashire in Britain – a county famous for its rain. Towneley set up a rain-collector on the roof of his hall, with a pipe to bring the rainwater into his bedroom window so that he could measure it accurately. Carefully-recorded weather measurements from the past, like Towneley's, are very important for modern meteorologists who need to know what the weather was like centuries ago in order to see whether the climate is changing. Today more than 5000 people in Britain have their own rain-gauges and make regular measurements.

RAIN OF BLOOD

If you're bored with colourless rain and pure white snow, keep a look out for red rain and black snow. They both occasionally fall. When red rain fell in Melbourne, Australia, people called it a 'rain of blood' because it coloured the countryside and stained their clothes a deep red. In Britain red rain sometimes falls a few days after winds have whipped up sandstorms in the Sahara desert. Grains of sandy dust get lifted into the atmosphere and carried northwards by the wind, until they are washed down to Earth as coloured raindrops. Ten million tonnes of red African dust landed on Britain in two days in 1903, according to one estimate. Black snow happens in a similar way, when dirt from smoky cities – or even distant volcano eruptions – gets into the snowflakes.

FALLING FISH ...

It rained fish at Sunderland, in the North of England, in August 1918. Hundreds of tiny fish fell to the ground during a thunderstorm. And in a town in Louisiana, USA, people were hit by falling fish as they went to work one day in October 1947. Some of the fish were as much as 23 centimetres long. In fact showers of fish have been reliably reported so often over the centuries that it seems they really do happen – though no one has explained how so many fish get sucked up into the sky in the first place. Sometimes the fish are freezing cold when they hit the ground, but there are no reports of showers of frozen fish fingers. And it has never *really* rained cats and dogs either – so far.

... AND RAINING REPTILES

A hailstone with a turtle inside fell in Mississippi, USA, in 1930, according to a report written at the time. The turtle was 20 centimetres long and covered all over in ice. In England, hundreds of tiny frogs were seen to fall to the ground in Wiltshire during a heavy shower in 1939. And in

Memphis, Tennessee, there was a very bad day in 1877 for people who don't like snakes: thousands of the reptiles – up to 40 centimetres long and still wriggling – apparently fell from the sky. If these reports are true (and there are plenty of others too), then scientists have still got some explaining to do.

FREEZING RAIN

No electricity for six weeks, in the middle of winter in one of the world's coldest countries – that's what people in parts of Canada had to endure when the 'Great Ice Storm' struck in January 1998.

Heavy rain followed by a vicious frost meant that electric power cables were coated with so much ice they snapped under the weight. Four million people were left in the dark, and fourteen thousand soldiers had to be brought in to deal with the emergency.

Ice storms, when rain is followed by frost, are some of the most dangerous weather conditions. Roads and pavements turn into skating rinks, and hospitals soon fill up with people with broken arms and legs.

CHEMICALS FROM THE SKY

On 10 April 1974, acid stronger than vinegar fell from the sky in Scotland, when a storm brought a bad attack of 'acid rain'. Normal rainwater is only very slightly acid, but sometimes pollution in the air turns it into 'acid rain'. Chemicals, such as carbon dioxide and nitrogen oxides, escape into the air when fossil fuels are burnt in vehicles and power stations. These chemicals turn into acids and dissolve in the tiny drops of water that form clouds. Eventually acid rain falls from the clouds, and can do serious damage to trees and kill fish when it collects in

lakes. Because clouds travel a long way, the acid rain often does damage in a different country from the one that produced the pollution. These days, governments in many countries are trying to make sure that less of the acid-making gases are allowed to get into the atmosphere.

BLAME THE BISHOP

A downpour in the year AD 971 started one of the best known 'weather sayings' – the one that says 'if it rains on St Swithin's Day (15 July), it will rain for the next forty days'. St Swithin was a Bishop of Winchester.

When he died in the year 862, he was buried outside the cathedral – as he had wished – so that rain could fall on his grave.

Later, in 971, a big ceremony was planned, when his remains would be moved to a new burial-place inside the cathedral. But after weeks of dry weather the day chosen for the ceremony, 15 July, was marked by a tremendous rainstorm (and followed by 40 days of rain if you believe some versions of the story).

WORSE TO COME

Of course no one believes the weather will really do exactly what the St Swithin story predicts, but apparently there is a grain of truth in the old saying. By 15 July in a typical year, the weather has often settled down into its pattern for the summer, so a fine 15 July could mean we're in for a good summer, and a wet 15 July could mean an unsettled one.

There are plenty of other 'Saints Day' predictions as well as the St Swithin one. For example 'if it freezes on St Matthias' Day (24 February), it will freeze for the next month', or 'if the sun shines on Pancake Day, it will shine every day until Easter'. One expert has even worked out that there are so many predictions about non-stop rain that if they all came true it would go on raining for ever!

SNOWMAN

When William Bentley was a boy his mother showed him a snow crystal through a microscope. The young American was so amazed that he spent 45 years in the mountains of New England photographing snow crystals.

When he died in 1931 he left 6000 beautiful photographs, no two of them alike. Snow crystals form when water vapour in cold air turns straight to ice. They all have a six-sided shape, but as it grows each crystal develops its own detailed structure of tiny needles. And because all snow crystals grow in slightly different conditions, they all end up different (though you would need a powerful microscope and a lot of patience to spot the difference between two that formed under similar conditions).

Incidentally in Britain we seldom see separate snow crystals. They usually stick together in bunches to form the larger lumps we call snowflakes.

ACCORDING TO LUKE

Where can you see a heap, a layer and a wisp? Answer: in the sky. They're all the names of types of cloud, except that meteorologists use Latin words instead of English. 'Cumulus' (a heap) describes lumpy cotton-wool clouds. 'Stratus' (a layer) is the name for flat sheets of cloud, and 'cirrus' (a wisp) describes feathery clouds. An English meteorologist called Luke Howard chose these names in 1803, together with another Latin word, 'nimbus', to describe the sort of clouds that rain comes from. Often the words are joined in pairs. For example, 'cumulonimbus' – usually shortened to 'cu-nim' – is the name for the bubbly flat-bottomed clouds that produce rain-showers.

IN A CLOUD

Clouds and fog are made up of water droplets so small you would have to collect ten billion of them to make a teaspoonful of water. In a normal cloud there are a few thousand of these tiny droplets in every matchboxful of air.

Clouds and fog are really the same thing. Fog is just a cloud that has formed down near the ground, and if you've ever flown through a cloud in an aeroplane you'll know that being inside a cloud is just like being in fog. But until two hundred years ago, nobody was sure what clouds are made of. Some scientists thought they were collections of very small bubbles floating in the air.

MOUNTAIN GHOST

Climbers on the Brocken Mountain in Germany are sometimes amazed to see a terrifying ghostly shape rising out of the mist in front of them. According to legend, one climber was so alarmed by the sight that he fell from a precipice and was killed. Actually there's nothing spooky about this ghostly shape.

It's just the climber's own shadow projected on to a bank of cloud when the sun is low in the sky, and it's been seen in many other places as well as the German mountain. Called the 'Brocken Spectre', the giant shadow is often surrounded by coloured rings. You can tell it's just a shadow because when the climber waves their arms, the spectre waves back.

FROM A CLEAR BLUE SKY

It only rains when it's cloudy – true or false? The answer is 'false' – rain or drizzle falling from a clear blue sky has been reported several times. And it's quite common for snow flakes to appear from nowhere on very cold days.

Probably this mysterious rain or snow happens when water vapour in the air turns straight into raindrops or ice crystals without becoming a cloud on the way. A more way-out theory is that the water comes from outer space, when watery meteorites or bits of comets hit the upper atmosphere. Either way, if someone says it rained or snowed when there was blue sky overhead, they may not be as crazy as they seem.

WEIGHING CLOUDS

An average-sized cloud weighs about the same as a jumbo jet. Think about one of those fluffy cotton-wool clouds you often see on fine days in summer. There's probably 500 tonnes of water in it – a little more than the weight of a large jet airliner. But clouds don't have wings, so what keeps them up? Part of the answer is that the cloud is made of very small droplets of water, and these droplets are so light that air resistance makes them fall to the ground very very slowly. Another part of the answer is that clouds often form on top of thermals – places where there is a current of air rising steadily upwards. So the cloud is being raised by the thermal just as fast as its droplets are sinking downwards. A really big thundercloud can weigh as much as 100,000 jumbo jets.

DUSTY RAINDROPS

Every drop of rain that falls has at least one grain of dust inside it. Raindrops start life in clouds, which are made up of millions of tiny water droplets or ice crystals – so small and light that they only fall to the ground very slowly. But these droplets or crystals can't form in pure clean air; they need a speck of dust to start them off, called a 'condensation nucleus'. Sometimes the dust is a grain of salt, which then dissolves in the water of the droplet. Once the tiny droplet has formed round a speck of dust, it grows and joins up with other droplets until it's heavy enough to fall to the ground as a raindrop. There's usually no shortage of dust in the atmosphere, which is why clouds seem to form so easily and it rains so often.

MAKING RAIN?

Scientists have tried to make rain by flying through clouds in aeroplanes, pouring out a trail of tiny crystals. The aim is to help farmers by providing more water to help their crops grow. The crystals are usually dry ice (frozen carbon dioxide gas) or a substance called silver iodide, and are supposed to turn the cloud into snow, which soon melts to form rain. The method is rather unreliable. Sometimes it does seem to make more rain, but sometimes it has the opposite effect and makes less rain than usual. And when it does work successfully it may cause trouble because next-door farmers claim that their own rain has been hijacked by someone else.

ANSWER TO PRAYER

Over the years, many people have tried to make rain by doing special dances, or by saying prayers. But these methods don't seem to be any more reliable than the scientific ones. In Sydney, Australia, in 1965 aboriginal people were brought in to end a drought by doing their rainmaking ritual. At the end of it the aborigines sat back in their air-conditioned hotel rooms, drank chilled beer, and waited. But no rain came, and the next day was just as hot and dry as before.

In Michigan, USA, in 1908 farmers held prayer meetings to try to save their crops from drought. The result was that it rained so hard that floods washed the crops away!

DESPERATE MEASURES

If the prayers and the dancing didn't work, people have tried all sorts of desperate measures to try to conjure up rain. In Russia, groups of peasant-women got their priest to put on all his special ceremonial robes and then poured water all over him, while others grabbed the nearest passing stranger and pushed him into a river. In Europe, Christians tried turning their statues of St Joseph upside down, while in South America the native people did horrid things to frogs. All these rituals probably made the people who did them feel better – but none of them produced a single drop more rain.

WHERE THE RAINBOW ENDS

Go to the place where a rainbow touches the ground. Dig a hole there, and you're sure to find a pot full of gold. That's what the old story says – but what's the catch? Everybody knows that to see a rainbow you must have rain and sun at the same time. Sunlight is caught by raindrops, split up into colours, and reflected back so you can see it. Often the rainbow is far away, but sometimes you may be lucky enough to see one that ends in your own back garden. The trouble starts when you try to get to the place where the rainbow ends. When you arrive there you find the rainbow has always vanished or moved on to somewhere further away. However far you go you can never catch up with it, which is why people who want impossible things are sometimes called 'rainbow-chasers'.

Quiz

1 Enough rain falls every day to give everyone on Earth
a) A thimbleful
b) A glassful
c) A hundred bathtubsful

2 Why does red rain occasionally fall?
a) When the water comes from the Red Sea
b) When sand from the desert gets mixed in with it
c) After there's been a red sunset

3 Which of these has *not* been reported falling with the rain?
a) Cats and dogs
b) Snakes
c) Small fish

4 Acid rain only falls...
a) When the atmosphere is badly polluted
b) Over chemical factories
c) At Glastonbury

5 What shape are snow crystals, usually?
a) Square with the corners chopped off
b) Round with knobs on
c) Six-sided with tiny needles

6 What are clouds made of?
a) Frozen air
b) Tiny drops of water (or ice)
c) Cotton wool

7 A cirrus cloud is
a) Feathery
b) Lumpy
c) Full of rain

8 Why do clouds stay up?
a) They're lighter than air
b) They're fixed to the sky
c) They're made of tiny droplets that only fall very slowly

9 Scientists try to make rain fall by
a) Turning statues upside down
b) Pouring crystals out of aeroplanes
c) Beating drums very loudly

10 According to legend, if you go to where a rainbow ends, you will find
a) A meteorologist
b) A pot of gold
c) The Wizard of Oz

CHAPTER 5

Storm Warning

Of all the tricks the weather plays, the big storms are the ones we remember best. With their violent winds and lashing rain they can be exciting, but often frightening and dangerous too.

Hurricanes are the biggest storms of all, lasting for days and spreading devastating winds and torrential rain over huge areas of land and sea. They make thousands of people homeless and do damage that costs billions of pounds to repair.

The wet and windy spells we have in Britain, called 'lows' or 'depressions', are similar to hurricanes but smaller and much less violent.

Tornadoes are just as dramatic – and dangerous – as hurricanes, but affect a much smaller area, sometimes just a few metres across. They can appear suddenly and be gone a few minutes later, leaving a trail of destruction behind them.

But it's thunderstorms that have always frightened people most. We feel small and powerless against their mighty flashes and bangs. Lightning can be a killer, and we can never be sure where it's going to strike next. No wonder people thought that thunderstorms meant the gods were angry.

STORM FORCE TEN

If whole trees are uprooted and buildings are damaged then you're in the middle of a Force 10 storm. But if the leaves on the trees are rustling gently it's just a Force 2 breeze. Force 10 and Force 2 are numbers on the Beaufort Wind Scale, invented by Admiral Beaufort in 1805 to help sailors record the strength of the wind at sea. The scale lets people estimate the speed of the wind, simply by looking at what effect it has. Its modern version is still sometimes used today, and goes from Force 0 (calm – smoke rises vertically) to Force 12 (hurricane – widespread severe damage).

WICKED WEATHER

In 1957 Audrey killed 550 people in America. In 1992 Andrew did 26 billion dollars worth of damage. And in 1998 Mitch made five million people homeless. But Audrey, Andrew and Mitch were not human villains. They were hurricanes – some of the most violent storms to hit the Americas in recent years. Hurricanes are huge whirling weather systems that can last for several days and bring devastating winds of more than 200 kilometres per hour to large areas of country (unlike tornadoes which are very much smaller and normally only last a few minutes – *see* **Naked Hens**, *page 92*.) Hurricanes have different names in other parts of the world. In parts of the Pacific Ocean region they are known as 'typhoons', and in the Indian Ocean they are called 'cyclones'.

NAME THAT STORM

Since the 1950s, every hurricane to hit the United States has been given a name. At first only girls' names were used, but many people thought girls shouldn't get all the blame for the damage that hurricanes do, so now boys' and girls' names are used alternately.

The first hurricane each year has a name beginning with 'a', the next one 'b', and so on. For example the list of names for 1999 started with Arlene, Brett, Cindy, Dennis, Emily, Floyd, Gert, Harvey ... If a hurricane is specially violent its name goes on to the 'retired list'. That means the name will never be used again, because it would bring back bad memories for people whose homes were destroyed or who lost relations or friends in the hurricane.

EYE OF THE STORM

If you're ever caught in a hurricane, don't be fooled if the wind suddenly drops. You could be in the 'eye' of the storm, a small calm region at the centre of many hurricanes. After several hours of torrential rain and storm-force winds, the rain suddenly stops and the wind dies down. The sun might even shine. People are tempted to come out into the open and start clearing up the damage. But watch out! The storm is not over. A hurricane is a huge whirlpool of cloud, wind and rain, and the 'eye' is at the centre of it. Soon the sky will get darker, rain will start again, and the gales will return – except that now the wind will blow in the opposite direction to the way it blew before.

NAKED HENS

Chickens with no feathers are sometimes reported running around after a tornado has struck a farm. Tornadoes – also known as 'twisters' – are much smaller than hurricanes. They are funnels of twisting air that stretch down below clouds and produce extremely violent winds where they touch the ground. In the 1940s an American did experiments to find out how much wind is needed to blow the feathers off a chicken (he used dead chickens in these experiments). Apparently the wind produced by a tornado is more than enough to do the job. Another theory is that chickens are so scared when they see a tornado coming that they automatically shed their feathers as part of a panic reaction. Yet another theory is that the stories of featherless chickens are just exaggerated rumours, and that it never really happens!

BLOWN AWAY

In 1974 a tornado in Mississippi, USA, picked up three buses, lifted them over a two-metre high bank, and dropped them in nearby woodland. This is just one example of the amazing power of tornado winds to pick things up and carry them away. Tornadoes sometimes pick up loose bits of paper from houses they have blown apart, and drop them anything up to 150 kilometres away. In 1930 a man was carried more than a kilometre by a tornado, but died soon after he landed, and in 1915 hundreds of dead ducks fell out of the sky 40 kilometres away from the end of the track of a violent tornado. The twisting winds that perform these feats are usually concentrated on a very small area – a few hundred metres across – but can reach a speed of 800 kilometres per hour.

COUNTING THE COST

The money spent clearing up after all the weather-related disasters in the USA in the ten years up to 1998 could have bought three new umbrellas for every man, woman and child on Earth.

The total that Americans had to pay was 150 billion dollars. Hot dry weather led to 2.5 billion dollars-worth of fire damage in California in 1991, while frosts in Florida did 2 billion dollars-worth of damage to the fruit crop in 1985. Flood damage along the Mississippi River cost 5 billion dollars in 1995, while in 1988 a drought and heatwave cost 40 billion dollars and killed more than 5000 people. And then there were all those hurricanes and tornadoes. No wonder people talk about putting money aside for a rainy day!

TRAIL OF DAMAGE

Tornadoes don't just happen in America; we get them in Britain too. A notable one left a 100-kilometre trail of damage across central England in May 1950. More than 50 houses lost their roofs, wooden farm buildings were lifted up and smashed, phone and power lines were torn down and a bus was overturned. Luckily the only deaths were farm animals, not people. In 1971 another tornado pushed a hefty steam locomotive 50 metres along a railway track in Yorkshire. And in 1981, 105 tornadoes were reported on a single day. Like most British tornadoes these were small-scale ones, leaving a trail just a few metres wide. So it would be quite possible for one person's house to be damaged by a tornado, while their neighbours' on each side were untouched.

ILL WIND

If the wind hadn't blown so strongly in Greenland in 1911, the Titanic might not have sunk in 1912. As everyone knows, Titanic sank after hitting an iceberg – but why was the iceberg there?

Icebergs in the Atlantic Ocean are floating chunks of ice that break off from the Arctic ice sheet. Many of these chunks soon drift ashore and melt, but if the wind is unusually strong, new-born icebergs are blown out into an ocean current that will carry them southwards towards the shipping lines. Months later they appear near Newfoundland, exactly in the region where Titanic met her fate.

After the Titanic disaster, a special airborne 'Ice Patrol' was set up which keeps constant watch for icebergs and warns nearby ships.

END OF THE WORLD?

The Queen of England had to hide in the basement of her Palace when a violent storm struck the country in 1703. Queen Anne thought the basement was the safest place to be, because bits of the Palace were blowing down. The Great Storm of 1703 was probably even worse than the 'hurricane' of 1987 (*see below*). At sea, many ships were sunk by the strong winds, and more than a thousand sailors drowned. On land, hundreds of people were killed, including an important churchman, the Bishop of Bath and Wells, who died when a chimney came crashing through his bedroom ceiling. According to one writer who lived through the storm, many people though that the end of the world had come.

ONE-TREE TOWN

Fifteen million trees blew down in one night in a storm that hit Southern England in October 1987. At a place called Sevenoaks, six out of seven large oak trees were blown down, and people wondered whether the town should change its name!

Most people who can remember this storm call it 'The Hurricane' but officially it was only a 'vigorous depression'.

The sudden storm was a great embarrassment for the weather-forecaster Michael Fish. In his regular TV forecast he said 'there isn't going to be a hurricane', but a few hours later the fiercest gales for nearly 300 years were blowing.

Windows were broken, roofs torn off, and electric power lines brought down. Poor old Michael Fish hasn't been allowed to forget his blunder, because his wrong forecast was recorded and has been re-shown on TV many times.

WEATHER IN A SPIN

If you haven't a clue where you are on the Earth, checking which way the wind blows might help. If you're in the Northern Hemisphere the wind blows *anti-clockwise* round the bad-weather systems known as 'lows', but in the Southern Hemisphere it blows *clockwise*. You can check this by looking at the weather map in a newspaper. The different directions are caused by the spinning of the Earth.

The same sort of thing should happen with your bathwater. North of the equator it should make an anti-clockwise whirlpool as it runs down the plughole, but a clockwise one south of the equator. But it's very difficult to check whether this really happens. Many other things can set off the whirlpool in the wrong direction, like the exact shape of your bathtub, or which way you wiggled your big toe as you got out of the bath.

FIRE-STORM

Lighting a fire can start a storm – but only if the fire is a big one. Gale-force winds sometimes develop around a huge blaze, such as a forest fire, producing a 'fire-storm'. It starts because flames and smoke and hot air form a powerful upward current of air above the blaze. Because so much air goes up in this current, more air has to rush in at ground level, producing powerful whirling winds. Fire-storms can also be a horrifying feature of warfare, developing in cities where many buildings had been set alight by being bombed. A bombing raid on Dresden in Germany in 1945, for example, set off a fire-storm that destroyed the centre of the city and may have killed more than 100,000 people. The fire-storm winds were so strong that people trying to run away from the blaze were blown back into it.

THOR'S HAMMER

A red-bearded god rides across the sky in a chariot pulled by two goats, waving his huge hammer. The god is called Thor, and his hammer splits the sky, causing violent flashes and bangs. That's the story that people in Scandinavia used to tell, more than a thousand years ago, to explain how thunder and lightning happen. Thor sounds like a frightening character, but actually he was one of the more friendly gods. Today we have more scientific ways to explain thunder and lightning, but we still remember Thor because one of the days of the week is named after him – you can probably work out which one, even though the 'o' in his name has turned into a 'u'.

FLASHES AND BANGS

In the time it takes you to read this page, about five thousand flashes of lightning will happen. But don't worry, it's very unlikely any of them will be anywhere near you. Scientists have worked out that if you add up all the thunderstorms happening at any moment everywhere in the world, the answer would be about two thousand. That means more than a million flashes and bangs every day. Most of the thunderstorms happen in hot and humid places near the equator. For example people on the island of Java hear thunder rumbling almost every day of the year. But in Britain most people only hear thunder on less than twenty days a year, and the chance of being caught in a violent thunderstorm is even less.

STRIKE ME DOWN!

Many people are terrified of lightning, but if you live in Britain the chance you'll actually be struck and killed by lightning this year is less than one in ten million. (This is about the same as the chance you'll win the lottery jackpot this week if you buy one ticket.) Your chance of being killed by lightning will be even less if you take sensible precautions. If you're caught out in a thunderstorm, stay inside a car or low building if you can. If that's not possible, crouch down in a hollow in the ground, or under a hedge or group of low bushes. Keep away from tall trees because they're the ones most likely to be struck. And don't play golf when there's thunder about – more people are struck by lightning on golf courses than anywhere else!

DON'T TRY THIS

A very important American risked instant death when he did an experiment to find out what lightning is. In 1752 Benjamin Franklin wanted to know if the electricity in a thundercloud was the same as the electricity he made in experiments in his laboratory. So when he saw a thundercloud approaching he flew a kite up into it. Electricity flowed down the wet kite-string into Franklin's apparatus on the ground – proving that lightning and normal electricity are the same thing. Franklin survived this risky experiment, and later helped write the famous Declaration of Independence, when America split off to become a separate country from Great Britain. The next person to try an experiment with a thunder-cloud was a Russian professor, but he wasn't so lucky. He was struck by lightning and killed.

SPOOKY GLOW

Trees in a forest sometimes glow with a spooky blue-green light when there's a thunderstorm around. The same glow – called a corona – is also seen on church spires, ship's masts, and even parts of aeroplanes. Sometimes a crackling or fizzing noise is heard with it. The glow happens when static electricity builds up on a wet surface and escapes into the damp air. Sailors used to call it 'St Elmo's fire' and thought it brought good luck. When their ship glowed with St Elmo's fire it meant the Saint would take good care of them.

BALL OF FIRE?

Imagine you are sitting at home during a thunderstorm. Suddenly a fuzzy glowing ball, as bright as a light bulb, comes through the window, even though the window is closed. The mysterious object is about the size of a football, and slowly moves across the room for a few seconds.

Over the years, hundreds of people have seen this strange phenomenon. Scientists call it 'ball lightning', but they can't explain what it is (and some scientists aren't sure it really exists at all). No one has ever managed to catch it, because the glowing ball always vanishes after a few seconds. So keep your eyes open next time there's a thunderstorm. You might be one of the lucky few people to witness something that has baffled scientists for years.

Quiz

1 Which of these is *not* another name for a hurricane?
a) Cyclone
b) Typhoon
c) Hurdy-gurdy

2 According to the rules for naming hurricanes, hurricane Greta could be followed by
a) Hurricane Rita
b) Hurricane Horace
c) Hurricane Hannah

3 In the eye of a hurricane, what should you do?
a) Start clearing up the damage
b) Start celebrating
c) Stay safe and wait for it to restart

4 Which of these have tornadoes been reported to do?
a) Lift buses
b) Blow the feathers off chickens
c) Push a steam locomotive along

5 In the Great Storm of 1703, Queen Anne
a) Hid in the basement
b) Went back to bed
c) Left the country

6 Compared to Europe, the wind in Australia
a) Is always colder
b) Is always stronger
c) Blows the other way round weather systems

7 Who or what is 'Thor'?
a) A god with a hammer
b) A goat with a red beard
c) What makes the snow melt

8 Over the whole world, how many thunderstorms are happening right now?
a) One or two
b) About a hundred
c) About two thousand

9 Which is the safest policy if you're caught out in a thunderstorm?
a) Climb a tree
b) Crouch in a hollow
c) Start a round of golf

10 What causes 'St Elmo's fire'?
a) A build-up of static electricity
b) Sailors drinking too much rum
c) St Elmo lighting a match

CHAPTER 6

Changing Climate

People sometimes complain that the weather is never the same two days running, and in Britain that's often true. Looking back in history we find that the weather's not the same two centuries running either. Two hundred years ago, for example, Britain's climate was cooler, on average, than it is today.

Scientists have developed ways of finding what the climate was like thousands, and even millions, of years ago. The results are quite alarming, showing that the world's climate patterns change from time to time for no apparent reason. Over the last six hundred million years there have been several of the freezing spells known as Ice Ages.

With the climate so variable, it's hard to predict the future climate. And the job's not made any easier by all the pollution we're now pumping into the atmosphere. Scientists argue about whether the weather will get warmer or cooler in the years ahead because of this. But almost everyone agrees that we are taking a risk. If all that extra carbon dioxide *does* lead to serious global warming it could be a catastrophe for the whole human race.

THE GREAT RAINS

Four billion years ago there were no oceans on the Earth. Then it rained and rained, and over millions of years the oceans filled up. In its early days the Earth was so hot that any water on its surface would have quickly boiled away. Then, as the surface cooled down, clouds formed and the great rains began. Probably most of the water that's now in the oceans originally fell from the sky as boiling hot rain, but some of it may have bubbled up from inside the Earth. Scientists aren't sure of the details because it all happened long before there were any humans – or any other forms of life – to observe what was going on.

THANK YOU, BACTERIA

If you go back three billion years in a time machine, don't breathe the air. At that time the Earth was much younger than it is now, and there was hardly any oxygen in the atmosphere. So you would soon suffocate if you stepped outside your time machine for a breath of fresh air. Scientists believe that much of the oxygen we breathe today was produced long ago by a special sort of bacteria that lived in the sea. These bacteria got energy from sunlight which they used to change carbon dioxide gas into oxygen – like green plants do today. Without their oxygen-producing efforts millions of years ago, we wouldn't be here at all!

NASTY WEATHER FOR DINOSAURS

Bad weather may have helped wipe out the dinosaurs. Some scientists believe the Earth turned cold and gloomy after it was hit by an asteroid 66 million years ago. The asteroid was a rock, about 10 kilometres wide, hurtling down at a speed of hundreds of thousands of kilometres per hour. When it hit the Earth the asteroid threw a huge cloud of dust up into the atmosphere. This dust spread all round the world and changed the climate, keeping out much of the Sun's heat and light. Plants could not grow properly, so plant-eating dinosaurs had little food, and starved to death. With plant-eating dinosaurs in short supply, the meat-eaters began to starve also. Other scientists believe that the meteorite impact, if it really happened, was only one of several factors that led to the downfall of the dinosaurs.

UNDER ICE

A million years ago, the place where you live was covered all year round with a thick layer of ice. That's true if you live in the northern parts of Britain, but not if you live in the south. In the last great Ice Age a huge sheet of permanent ice built up from compressed snow, and spread out from the Arctic to cover much of Europe and North America. In Britain the ice reached down roughly to the Bristol Channel and the Thames Estuary. South of there, the ground was permanently frozen solid, but not ice-covered. There have been several ice ages over the last six hundred million years. The most recent one only ended when the weather warmed up about ten thousand years ago.

ICE PLANET

Even today there is six times more ice on our planet than there is air. Almost all this ice is locked up in two enormous ice-sheets, in Antarctica and Greenland, where the ice is two kilometres thick on average. Altogether it adds up to 30 quadrillion tonnes of ice (or 30,000,000,000,000,000 tonnes if you prefer), which is six times more than the weight of the whole atmosphere. In fact there's enough ice to provide everyone on Earth with a hundred ice lollies every day for the next million years. If all this ice melted it would raise sea level all over the world by almost enough to completely submerge Big Ben in London. All this ice originally fell from the sky in the form of snowflakes. The snow built up over hundreds of thousands of years, and gradually got crushed into solid ice as more and more snow fell on top of it.

ANCIENT CLIMATE

Meteorologists can find how the climate has changed in the past by drilling deep holes in the ice sheet. They see layers in the ice – one for each year – so by counting back they can find which layer of ice, deep down below the surface, fell as snow, say, ten thousand years ago. Then they do careful tests on the tiny bubbles of air inside this ancient ice which tell them whether it was a warm year or a cold year when that particular layer formed. The results are surprising, because they show that the long-term weather is unsteady, with global warming and global cooling happening quite often – long before there was any human pollution that might cause the climate to change.

WALKING THE CHANNEL

Ten thousand years ago you could walk from Dover to Calais (except that Dover and Calais didn't exist then of course). At that time the Ice Age was just ending, but so much water was still locked up in the huge ice sheets covering much of the world that the level of water in the sea was much lower than it is now – so low that parts of the English Channel had no water in them at all. Then as the ice melted, water flowed back into the oceans, so that 8000 years ago the British Isles were once again cut off from the rest of Europe. After that, nobody walked across the Channel until the 1990s, when a few people were allowed to tramp right through the new Channel Tunnel before the trains began to run through it.

ICE QUEEN

The Queen of England once walked right across the River Thames – but not on a bridge. Between the years 1407 and 1665 there were six winters so cold that the Thames froze over, and it was during one of these that Queen Elizabeth I led her courtiers in a slow procession across the ice. In some winters the ice was so thick that carts and wagons could be driven on to it, and the people of London sometimes celebrated with 'Frost Fairs' held on the ice. For several centuries, until about 1850, Europe was in the grip of a 'Little Ice Age' when the weather was a little colder, on average, than it is today.

Nowadays the Thames never freezes over, partly because the weather is warmer, but mainly because the river has been made narrower, by building up its banks, so that the water is deeper and flows much faster.

WORST SUMMER

The worst summer in the last 600 years happened in 1601. According to one writer, 'the month of June was very colde, with frosts every morning'. The reason for the awful weather was a volcano in Peru which had erupted the year before. It sent millions of tonnes of dust into the atmosphere, which spread like a veil around the world and cut out some of the sun's warmth.

Scientists discover which years were cold by cutting down old trees and looking at the tree rings inside them. Trees make a new ring every year, and the thickness of the ring depends on what the weather was like in that particular year. Unusually cold years like 1601 have very narrow rings. Another year that was badly affected by volcano dust was 1816, known as 'the year without a summer' by the unfortunate people who had to live through it.

RED SKY AT NIGHT

When a volcano erupted in Indonesia in 1883, people in England saw brilliant red sunsets for months afterwards. The volcano, Krakatau, sent millions of tonnes of dust into the upper atmosphere, where it soon spread all around the world, and it was this dust that affected the sun's rays to produce the beautiful sunsets. Krakatau had another effect that was not so welcome; all that dust in the atmosphere stopped some of the sun's warmth getting through, and the weather in many parts of the world was colder than usual for several years afterwards. Incidentally Krakatau's eruption was 26 times more violent than the most powerful hydrogen bomb ever tested. The bang it made was so loud it could be heard in Australia, nearly 5000 kilometres away.

SUNSPOTS

When the Sun gets spottier the Earth gets hotter, according to some people. Sunspots are darker patches on the Sun's surface that usually last a few days. Every 11 years there is a 'sunspot maximum' when the Sun is at its spottiest. In between the maxima are periods when the Sun has fewer spots. Many people have tried to discover changes on the Earth, such as the average temperature or even the ups and downs of the stock exchange, that might keep step with the changes in numbers of sunspots.

Some scientists claim that the Earth tends to be hotter at times of sunspot maxima, but other scientists think this hasn't been definitely proved. If it *is* true, it's good news for the new millennium, because the year 2001 is a sunspot maximum.

BLAME THE JET STREAM

A twice-hurricane-force wind could be blowing above your head at this very moment. Narrow bands of very strong wind, known as jet streams, blow from east to west right round the world, at a height of about ten kilometres above the ground. One of these jet streams blows across the North Atlantic and often passes over Britain. Jet aircraft use it to speed up their crossing from America to Europe, and avoid it when they go the other way. Jet stream winds can reach speeds as high as 500 kilometres per hour. They play a big part in deciding what sort of weather we get down below. For example, the cool wet summer we had in Britain in 1998 can be blamed on the jet stream, which moved further south than usual that year.

LAZY DAYS

It's official: days don't just *seem* longer when the weather's bad, they really *are* longer – but only by less than a thousandth of a second. Scientists have used radio telescopes to measure the Earth's rotation very accurately. They find that when the atmosphere speeds up, because of the strong winds that go with some large-scale weather systems, the Earth slows down. And because a day is the time it takes the Earth to rotate once, slower rotation means a longer day. It's all because of something called 'angular momentum'. There's only a fixed amount of it available, and if the atmosphere is moving fast it takes more than its usual share of angular momentum. Then there's less left for the Earth, so it has to rotate a tiny bit slower than usual. When the strong winds die down, the Earth returns to normal.

SUMMER AND WINTER

The Earth is 5 million kilometres nearer to the Sun in January than it is in July. That is because the Earth's orbit round the Sun isn't an exact circle, but a sort of oval called an ellipse. So why do we get the coldest weather (in the Northern Hemisphere) at the time when we're closest to the Sun? The answer is because the Earth's axis of spin is tilted, and this has a much bigger effect than the change of distance from the Sun. It means that in the Northern Hemisphere the Sun beats down on us from much higher in the sky in July than it does in January. If the Earth's axis wasn't tilted, all four seasons would be the same, except that it would be very slightly warmer everywhere on Earth in January, when we're slightly nearer the Sun, than in July – so perhaps that's when everyone on Earth would take their 'summer' holidays.

CHILLY OUTLOOK?

'Cooler and cooler, with a lot more frost and snow'. That's a weather forecast for Britain for the next twenty thousand years. Scientists make the prediction by studying how the Earth's orbit round the Sun changes slightly over thousands of years, and the way its axis of rotation changes its tilt – like a wobbly spinning top. These changes mean that Britain won't get quite so much warmth from the Sun in years to come. But like all forecasts, this one could be wrong – particularly if the Earth's climate is affected by all the carbon dioxide gas that humans are putting into the atmosphere (*see* **Blanket of gas**, *page 43*).

GLOBAL CHILLING

Global warming could make Britain colder, not hotter, because it might make the Gulf Stream pack up. The Gulf Stream is a warm-water current in the Atlantic Ocean that flows towards the British Isles, bringing as much heat as 27,000 power stations could supply. This makes our climate much warmer than it would otherwise be. Global warming could change the pattern of ocean currents and cut off this supply of free heat. If that happened, according to some scientists, the average temperature in Britain would drop by 5 °C, which doesn't sound a lot, but would be enough to make the average temperature in Britain similar to what Iceland has today.

Quiz

1 The oxygen in the Earth's atmosphere was made by
a) Cavemen
b) Beetles
c) Bacteria

2 Scientists think the dinosaurs may have died out because
a) A comet poisoned the Earth
b) An asteroid changed the climate
c) They couldn't be bothered to eat

3 Which region was *not* frozen over in the last age?
a) Scotland
b) Yorkshire
c) Kent

4 How much ice is there on the Earth today?
a) Ten billion tonnes
b) Twenty trillion tonnes
c) Thirty quadrillion tonnes

5 Ten thousand years ago you could
a) Walk across the English Channel
b) Skate across the English Channel
c) Drive through the Channel Tunnel

6 Queen Elizabeth I is remembered for
a) Inventing ice hockey
b) Walking on the ice in London
c) Eating a lot of ice cream

7 What caused the bad summer in Britain in the year 1601?
a) An earthquake in Australia
b) A forest fire in China
c) A volcano in Peru

8 Aeroplanes cross quicker from America to Europe than the other way because
a) The jet stream helps them
b) It's not so far to go
c) British pilots can't wait to get home

9 The distance from the Earth to the Sun is
a) Smallest in January
b) Smallest in July
c) The same all year round

10 Britain's future climate will be
a) Cooler than now
b) Warmer than now
c) Nobody really knows

Quiz Answers

CHAPTER 1

1 - b, 2 - c, 3 - a, 4 - c, 5 - b,
6 - b, 7 - b, 8 - c, 9 - a, 10 - b

CHAPTER 2

1 - c, 2 - a, 3 - b, 4 - b,
5 - c (and perhaps b), 6 - b, 7 - c,
8 - c 9 - a, 10 - a

CHAPTER 3

1 - c, 2 - b, 3 - c, 4 - b,
5 - a (and possibly also c), 6 - b, 7 - a,
8 - c, 9 - a, 10 - c

CHAPTER 4

1 - c, 2 - b, 3 - a, 4 - a, 5 - c,
6 - b, 7 - a, 8 - c, 9 - b, 10 - b

CHAPTER 5

1 - c, 2 - b, 3 - c, 4 - a, b, and c,
5 - a, 6 - c, 7 - a, 8 - c, 9 - b, 10 - a

CHAPTER 6

1 - c, 2 - b, 3 - c, 4 - c, 5 - a,
6 - b, 7 - c, 8 - a, 9 - a, 10 - c

Index